New Plants

Developed at
Lawrence Hall of Science
University of California at Berkeley

Published and Distributed by **Delta Education**

ISBN 1-58356-478-0

542-1338

2 3 4 5 6 7 8 9 10 MPC 06 05 04 03 02 01

Table of Contents

What Do Plants Need?

Many people grow plants. They grow plants
in clay pots and window boxes. They grow
plants in gardens and on farms. Some
people grow plants to sell. People who grow
plants know what plants need to live.

Plants need water. They take up water through their roots. Water travels from the roots to the stems and leaves.

Plants need nutrients.
Nutrients come from the soil.
They are mixed in the water
that travels through the plants.

Plants need light. Leaves capture sunlight
to make food for the plants. The food
allows the plants to grow. Plants can store
some of the food to use later.

Plants need space. Roots need room
to grow. Roots can't get enough
water and nutrients if they are too
crowded. Leaves that are too
crowded can't get enough light.

Do you think this plant will have
what it needs to grow big and strong?

How Seeds Travel

One way to give plants enough
space is to get rid of weeds.
Weeds are unwanted plants.

How did weeds get into this garden?

Like many plants, weeds start as seeds. Seeds come from a plant's flower. When the seeds are ripe, they are ready to travel.

Some seeds float or spin through the air. They may land far from where they started. If they land on moist soil, they may start to grow.

Some seeds hitch rides on animals.
These seeds have little hooks. The hooks
hold the seeds to an animal's fur. The
seeds go where the animal goes.

Seeds can even hitch a ride
on you! They can stick to your
sweater or shoes. When you brush
the seeds off, they might land
on soil and grow.

Some seeds are moved by
birds and squirrels. Birds
eat berries. Inside the
berries are seeds. The seeds
pass through the bird. They
are left in a new place in
the bird's droppings.

Squirrels eat seeds, too.
They bury acorns to eat
during the winter.
In the spring, forgotten
acorns begin to grow
into oak trees.

Now you know many
ways that seeds travel.
How do you think
the weeds got into
the garden on page 8?

The Story of Wheat

People use plants in many ways. They make clothing, furniture, and houses from plants. They also use plants for food.

Wheat is an important food plant. For thousands of years, people have used wheat to make flour. Flour is used in cooking and baking.

The story begins when farmers sow wheat seeds in big fields.

Before long, the seeds sprout. At first, the wheat looks like grass you might see in a lawn. The plants grow bigger and bigger. Then, on top of each wheat plant, new seeds grow. The seeds, called grain, ripen in the sun.

The wheat plants die and turn golden yellow. Now, the wheat grain is ready to harvest. The farmer drives a big combine over the field of wheat. The combine cuts the wheat. The combine separates the grain from the rest of the plant, too.

The grain is then put into large silos. It is kept there until it is sent to a mill for grinding. But farmers don't send all of their grain to the mill.

Why do you think they keep some of it?

At the mill, the grain is ground into flour.
The flour is put into sacks and packages
of different sizes. These are sent to
bakeries and grocery stores.

Flour is used in bakeries and in your home. It can be mixed with water and other things. The mixture might be baked in an oven or cooked on a stove. When it's finished, there is always something good to eat!

Bread, pasta, and tortillas can be made from flour.
Can you think of other things?

Plants around the World

Plants grow almost everywhere.
Some plants live in warm,
wet places like rain forests.

Rain forests have more kinds of
plants than anywhere else.
Some of the plants are very tall.
Some have very large leaves.

Plants grow in the tundra, where it is frosty and dry. The growing season in the tundra is short. Tundra plants must flower and make seeds before the cold weather comes again.

Plants grow in the dry, windy desert.
It doesn't rain very often in a desert.
Desert plants have special ways of
surviving.

Cactus plants have long roots. The roots
spread out just beneath the desert floor.
When it rains, the roots take in lots of
water. They store the water in their
thick stems.

There are lots of plants in temperate forests. In these forests, summers are warm and winters are cold. There is plenty of rain and snow.

Many trees in these forests lose their leaves in the fall. New leaves grow back in the spring.

Some parts of the world are covered by grass. Grasslands are warm in summer and cool in winter.

At the end of summer, the green grass turns golden and dies. Grass seeds fall to the ground. The seeds sprout when it is warmer and wetter again. The life cycle continues.

Some plants live in water. The roots of water lilies grow deep in the mud. At first, their leaves stay rolled up and under the water. Later, they grow to the surface and open up.

What kinds of plants grow where you live?

Glossary

Combine - a machine that cuts wheat and separates the grain.

Flour - a fine powder made from grinding wheat seeds.

Grain - a hard seed that grows at the top of a wheat plant.

Harvest - to gather in a crop, such as wheat.

Life cycle - the stages in the life of a plant. New plants come from older plants.

Nutrients - something living things need to grow and stay healthy.

Silo - a large tower that stores grain.

Sow - to plant a seed.

Tundra - treeless land in the arctic, or at high altitudes.

Wheat - a type of grass that makes seeds that can be ground into flour.